Refugee Resilience:
Elevating Lives, Communities, and America

Refugee Resilience:
Elevating Lives, Communities, and America

Contents

Refugee Resilience:
Elevating Lives, Communities, and America

professional before adopting any of the suggestions in this book or drawing inferences from it.

This publication reflects the author's views, experiences, and opinions. It is intended to provide helpful and informative material on the subjects addressed in the publication. The author and publisher shall have neither liability nor responsibility to any person or entity with respect to any loss, damage, or injury caused, or alleged to be caused, directly or indirectly by the information contained in this book.

While the author has made every effort to ensure the accuracy and completeness of the information contained in this publication, we assume no responsibility for errors, inaccuracies, omissions, or any inconsistency herein. Any slights of people or organizations are unintentional.

Introduction: Di Tran – A Refugee's Journey of Love, Gratitude, and Purpose

I was seven years old when my family and I arrived in the United States, fleeing the mud and poverty of rural Vietnam. We came with nothing but hope, a belief in the promise of America, and an unyielding determination to build a better future. My parents sacrificed everything—selling what little we had—to escape a life of hardship, stepping into the unknown with courage and faith.

When we landed on American soil, the challenges were immediate and overwhelming. We spoke no English, had no money, and knew no one. The first years were humbling; my family and I relied on government programs, the kindness of strangers, and community organizations to find our footing. I still remember standing in line at a food bank, clutching my mother's hand, while she whispered that this country would give us a chance if we worked hard enough. Those early years were tough, but they were also transformative.

It was through the United States' refugee resettlement programs that my family found housing,

Refugee Resilience:
Elevating Lives, Communities, and America

access to education, and the opportunity to work. These programs gave us the foundation we needed to survive, but it was the people—the neighbors, teachers, and mentors—who gave us the inspiration to thrive. America became more than just a refuge for my family; it became the home where our dreams could take root and flourish.

Today, as I write this, I am 42 years old—a proud Vietnamese-American who considers the United States the greatest country on earth. I am a product of this nation's refugee programs, a testimony to their effectiveness when coupled with hard work and resilience. I am also a witness to the extraordinary potential of refugees to enrich this nation—not just as contributors to the workforce but as creators, innovators, and stewards of its future.

My journey from being a struggling refugee to becoming a successful entrepreneur is not just my story—it is the story of what is possible in America. I am now the founder of **Di Tran Enterprise**, a unique organization that bridges the gap between refugees and this great country. We are a hybrid model of both profit and non-profit initiatives, dedicated to creating opportunities for immigrants and refugees to become productive, thriving members of society.

Refugee Resilience:
Elevating Lives, Communities, and America

The Message of Love and Gratitude

The foundation of my work is love—love for this country, love for the people it shelters, and love for the opportunities it provides. America has given me everything: a safe home, an education, and the chance to build something meaningful. For that, I am eternally grateful. This gratitude fuels my mission to help others, particularly refugees like myself, find their way to success and fulfillment in this great land.

Refugees arrive in America with dreams, determination, and resilience, but they also face immense barriers: language, housing, employment, and cultural integration. My mission is to bridge these gaps by creating systems that transform refugees from individuals in need into assets for this country. My vision is to help refugees not just survive but thrive, to enable them to give back to America as valued members of its workforce and communities.

Through **Di Tran Enterprise**, we have privately helped over 1,000 individuals to date, and this is just the beginning. From affordable housing to workforce development, from educational programs to community-building initiatives, we work tirelessly to ensure that refugees are not just supported but empowered. Every life we touch is a testament to the boundless potential of those who are given a chance.

Refugees as America's Strength

The common narrative often views refugees as a burden on the system, but I know firsthand that this could not be further from the truth. Refugees are among the most resilient, resourceful, and hardworking people you will ever meet. They arrive with the determination to rebuild their lives and the humility to start from nothing. When given the right opportunities, they contribute to their communities in extraordinary ways—as workers, business owners, taxpayers, and neighbors.

Through my work, I have seen refugees become salon owners, healthcare workers, skilled tradespeople, and more. They are not just employees but creators of jobs and value. They bring diversity, innovation, and cultural richness to every corner of this nation. By integrating refugees into America's employment system, we are not just helping individuals—we are strengthening the very fabric of this country.

Refugee Resilience:
Elevating Lives, Communities, and America

The programs we design at **Di Tran Enterprise** are aimed at creating long-term solutions: affordable housing to give families stability, skills training to make them employable, and community support to help them integrate. Refugees are not passive recipients of aid; they are active participants in building their own futures. And as they succeed, they enrich America in countless ways.

Di Tran Enterprise: Bridging the Gap

At **Di Tran Enterprise**, we believe in a simple yet powerful philosophy: every individual has value, and every challenge is an opportunity. Our organization is structured to bridge the gaps that often exist between refugees and the systems meant to support them.

On the **non-profit side**, we focus on immediate needs:

- Providing affordable housing for refugee families.

- Offering scholarships and tuition-free training programs in industries like beauty, healthcare, and technology.

Refugee Resilience:
Elevating Lives, Communities, and America

- Creating mentorship and coaching programs to help refugees navigate life in America.

On the **for-profit side**, we ensure sustainability and growth:

- Employing refugees in industries that match their skills while training them for higher-level opportunities.

- Partnering with businesses to create job opportunities tailored to refugee populations.

- Investing in real estate to ensure that housing remains affordable and accessible for those who need it most.

This hybrid model allows us to serve refugees holistically, addressing both their immediate needs and their long-term potential. We don't just provide services; we build pathways for refugees to become independent, successful, and giving members of society.

A Vision for the Future

I believe that **Di Tran Enterprise** is the perfect partner for the government to expand and enhance refugee assistance programs. Our approach is grounded in experience, driven by passion, and guided by results. We know what works because we live it every day.

Refugees are not problems to be solved; they are opportunities to be embraced. With the right support, they can become some of America's greatest assets, contributing to its economy, culture, and communities. By partnering with federal and state programs, **Di Tran Enterprise** can scale its impact, creating innovative solutions that empower refugees while strengthening the nation as a whole.

This is more than just a mission for me; it is my life's work. I am here because America gave me a chance, and now I want to give others that same chance. Together, we can create a system where refugees are not just welcomed but empowered to thrive. Together, we can build a stronger, more inclusive America—one life at a time.

This book is my invitation to the government, business leaders, and communities to join me in this mission. Let us take what I have learned through my journey and multiply its impact across the country. Let us celebrate America as the greatest nation on earth, not just for those born here but for those who

Refugee Resilience:
Elevating Lives, Communities, and America

come here seeking hope and opportunity. Let us transform refugees into a force for good, for themselves, for their communities, and for this nation we all call home.

Chapter 1: Refugee Journey – A Refugee's American Dream

When my family and I first arrived in the United States, we were burdened with uncertainty and an overwhelming sense of survival. We came with no English skills, no money, and no roadmap for what lay ahead. Our lives in Vietnam were defined by hardship, and though we left behind everything we knew, we carried hope in our hearts. Hope that America would not only shelter us but provide a pathway to a better life. This hope, shared by millions of refugees, is what sustains and propels those who seek refuge in the United States.

Every refugee's story is unique, yet there is a shared thread that binds us together: the universal desire to escape danger, rebuild our lives, and contribute to the communities that welcome us. From the Vietnamese boat people to Cuban exiles and beyond, America's history has been shaped by the resilience of refugees. The programs, policies, and partnerships that support them are the backbone of their survival and eventual success.

Refugee Resilience:
Elevating Lives, Communities, and America

This chapter explores the common struggles faced by refugees, the pivotal role of U.S. refugee assistance programs, and how organizations like **Di Tran Enterprise** partner with the government to bridge the gap between survival and thriving. Through my personal journey and examples of other refugee communities, we will examine how America remains the ultimate platform for growth and opportunity, and how we can collectively work to empower the next wave of hopeful arrivals.

My Journey as a Vietnamese Refugee

In the years following the Vietnam War, the country was in turmoil. My family, like many others, lived under harsh conditions that offered little hope for the future. My parents made the agonizing decision to leave everything behind, risking everything for a chance at freedom and opportunity.

We arrived in the United States in the early 1990s. I was just a child, and my first memory of America was both awe-inspiring and intimidating. The streets were wide, the buildings tall, and the language incomprehensible. I remember my parents clutching each other's hands, their faces a mixture of relief

Refugee Resilience:
Elevating Lives, Communities, and America

and fear. They had no English skills, no jobs, and no immediate support network.

In those early years, the government's refugee programs became our lifeline. Housing assistance ensured we had a roof over our heads. Public schools welcomed me despite my inability to speak English, patiently teaching me the language and helping me integrate. Community organizations provided food, clothing, and emotional support. These programs not only sustained us but also instilled in us a sense of hope that we were not alone.

Still, the challenges were immense. I was often embarrassed by my lack of English skills, and my parents worked long hours in low-paying jobs, barely making ends meet. But we were determined to persevere. My parents often reminded me, "America has given us a chance. Now it's up to us to make it count."

Over time, we found our footing. I graduated high school, went on to college, and eventually built a career in engineering before transitioning into entrepreneurship. The struggles my family faced shaped my values and ignited a passion to give back. I knew that if America could lift us from poverty and hardship, it could do the same for others.

Refugees as Resilient Contributors

The story of my family is not unique. Refugees from all corners of the world arrive in America carrying trauma, but also determination. Vietnamese refugees, often referred to as the "boat people," are a prime example. In the 1970s and 1980s, hundreds of thousands fled communist Vietnam in small, overcrowded boats, risking death at sea for a chance at freedom. Once in the U.S., they faced cultural and linguistic barriers, but their resilience enabled them to establish thriving communities. Today, Vietnamese-Americans are among the most successful immigrant groups in the country, contributing to industries ranging from healthcare to technology.

Similarly, Cuban refugees fleeing Fidel Castro's regime in the 1960s and 1970s found refuge in the United States, particularly in Florida. Programs like the Cuban Refugee Emergency Center provided immediate assistance, helping families find housing, employment, and language training. Over time, Cuban-Americans have become a vital part of the

Refugee Resilience:
Elevating Lives, Communities, and America

U.S. economy and culture, with leaders in politics, business, and the arts.

More recently, refugees from Syria, Afghanistan, and Ukraine have brought their own stories of survival and hope. These individuals arrive with diverse skills and perspectives, eager to rebuild their lives and contribute to the communities that welcome them. However, their journeys are often marked by significant challenges, including housing shortages, employment barriers, and the trauma of displacement.

How U.S. Refugee Programs Support Integration

The success of refugees in America is a testament to the strength of U.S. refugee assistance programs. Agencies like the Office of Refugee Resettlement (ORR) and partnerships with non-governmental organizations (NGOs) provide essential services, including:

1. **Housing Assistance**: Ensuring refugees have a safe place to live upon arrival.

2. **Employment Services**: Offering job placement, skills training, and career counseling.

3. **Language Training**: Teaching English to help refugees navigate their new environment.

4. **Healthcare Access**: Providing medical care to address immediate and long-term needs.

5. **Community Support**: Fostering integration through mentorship programs and cultural orientation.

These programs lay the foundation for refugees to transition from survival to self-sufficiency. However, they are often limited in scope and funding, which is where private organizations like **Di Tran Enterprise** play a crucial role.

Di Tran Enterprise: Bridging the Gap

As someone who has walked the path of a refugee, I understand the gaps in the system better than most. Government programs provide vital resources, but they often lack the cultural nuance, flexibility, and scalability needed to address the unique challenges refugees face. This is why I founded **Di Tran Enterprise**—to serve as a bridge between refugees and the opportunities that await them in America.

Refugee Resilience:
Elevating Lives, Communities, and America

Our model is simple yet impactful. We combine the resources of government programs with the agility of private enterprise to deliver holistic support for refugees. Some of our initiatives include:

- **Affordable Housing Projects**: Partnering with local governments to provide safe, stable homes for refugee families.

- **Workforce Development Programs**: Offering training and job placement in industries like healthcare, beauty, and technology.

- **Entrepreneurial Support**: Helping refugees start small businesses, inspired by my own journey as an entrepreneur.

- **Community Building**: Creating mentorship networks that connect refugees with local leaders and resources.

One example of our work is a partnership with a state housing agency to develop affordable housing specifically for refugees. By combining federal funding with private investment, we created a sustainable model that not only provides shelter but fosters community.

Refugee Resilience:
Elevating Lives, Communities, and America

Another initiative focuses on workforce integration. Through partnerships with local businesses and government grants, we've trained hundreds of refugees in high-demand industries, ensuring they have the skills needed to succeed in the U.S. economy. These programs do more than just place people in jobs; they empower refugees to become self-reliant contributors to society.

Empowering Refugees to Give Back

One of the greatest joys of my work is seeing refugees not just survive but thrive—and give back to the communities that welcomed them. I've watched refugees go from struggling to find their footing to becoming business owners, community leaders, and mentors for the next generation.

Take the story of Mai, a young Vietnamese refugee who arrived in the U.S. with her two children. Through our training programs, she earned her cosmetology license and eventually opened her own salon. Today, she employs five people, mentors other refugees, and actively volunteers in her community.

Refugee Resilience:
Elevating Lives, Communities, and America

Or consider Ahmed, an Afghan refugee who fled the Taliban with his family. With the help of our workforce development program, he found a job in construction and is now saving to buy his first home. He often says, "America saved my life, and now it's my turn to give back."

These stories are a testament to the transformative power of opportunity. Refugees are not burdens; they are assets waiting to be unlocked.

America: The Land of Opportunity

For me, America is more than a place—it is a promise. A promise that anyone, regardless of where they come from, can achieve their dreams through hard work and determination. This country took me in when I had nothing and gave me everything. It provided the platform for my growth and success, and I will never stop being grateful.

I often reflect on what makes America unique. It is not just the wealth or resources but the spirit of generosity and resilience that defines this nation. America's greatness lies in its ability to lift people up, to offer second chances, and to welcome those who seek refuge from a world that has failed them.

Refugee Resilience:
Elevating Lives, Communities, and America

As a Vietnamese refugee, I carry a deep love for this country. It has given me opportunities I could never have imagined, and it continues to inspire me to give back. Through **Di Tran Enterprise**, I hope to honor the promise of America by helping others achieve their own dreams.

This is the American Dream—not just for me but for every refugee who arrives on these shores. Together, we can build a future where refugees are not just beneficiaries but builders of a stronger, more inclusive America.

Chapter 2: Refugees in America – Challenges and Opportunities

The United States has long stood as a beacon of hope for those fleeing persecution, war, and hardship. Refugees arrive with a blend of optimism and uncertainty, eager to rebuild their lives while navigating a labyrinth of challenges. For decades, the government has worked tirelessly to provide resources for refugees through programs designed to support their resettlement and integration. However, the complexity of these challenges requires more than just government intervention—it demands a bridge between policy and people.

Di Tran Enterprise is uniquely positioned to be that bridge. With a mission rooted in love, resilience, and the belief that *"Yes I CAN"*, this organization is a perfect partner for government agencies seeking result-oriented solutions. By empowering refugees to become assets for America, **Di Tran Enterprise** not only transforms individual lives but also strengthens the communities they join. This chapter explores the challenges refugees face, the opportunities they bring, and how a multi-year strategic approach led

Refugee Resilience:
Elevating Lives, Communities, and America

by Di Tran Enterprise can elevate the U.S. refugee resettlement system to new heights.

The Realities Refugees Face Upon Arrival

Refugees enter the United States with little more than the clothes on their backs and the dreams in their hearts. While programs exist to assist them, the realities they face are daunting. These challenges often prevent refugees from reaching their full potential, limiting their ability to contribute to society effectively.

1. Housing Shortages

Finding safe, affordable housing is one of the most immediate challenges for refugees. Many arrive with limited financial resources and no credit history, making it difficult to secure housing in competitive markets. While government programs such as Section 8 housing vouchers provide some relief, the demand far exceeds the supply.

Di Tran Enterprise's Solution:
Di Tran Enterprise recognizes that stable housing is the foundation for success. Through partnerships with local governments and private investors, the organization develops affordable housing tailored to

refugee families. These projects not only provide immediate shelter but also create community hubs where refugees can access additional resources, such as job training and childcare services.

2. Language Barriers

Language is the gateway to integration. Without English proficiency, refugees struggle to navigate daily life, from understanding legal documents to communicating with employers. Language barriers often isolate refugees, delaying their ability to build relationships and find work.

Di Tran Enterprise's Solution:
Language training is a cornerstone of Di Tran Enterprise's strategy. By offering immersive English programs alongside vocational training, refugees can learn the language in a practical, job-oriented context. Additionally, the organization pairs refugees with bilingual mentors who guide them through their initial months in the U.S., ensuring they feel supported both personally and professionally.

3. Employment Struggles and Recognition of Skills

Refugee Resilience:
Elevating Lives, Communities, and America

While many refugees arrive with valuable skills, these are often unrecognized in the U.S. labor market. Doctors, engineers, and teachers from their home countries may find themselves working low-wage jobs due to licensing and certification barriers. This underutilization of talent represents a missed opportunity for both refugees and the economy.

Di Tran Enterprise's Solution:
Di Tran Enterprise bridges this gap through tailored workforce development programs. By collaborating with industry leaders and government agencies, the organization creates pathways for skill recognition and re-certification. For refugees with limited skills, Di Tran Enterprise provides job training in high-demand fields such as healthcare, technology, and beauty services. These programs are designed not only to place refugees in jobs but also to set them on a trajectory for long-term career growth.

Opportunities Refugees Bring to America

While the challenges are significant, the opportunities refugees bring to America are equally profound. Refugees contribute diverse skills, cultural wealth, and economic potential, making them invaluable to the nation's growth and prosperity.

Refugee Resilience:
Elevating Lives, Communities, and America

1. Diverse Skills

Refugees arrive with a wide range of skills and experiences. From artisans to scientists, they bring expertise that can enrich local industries and address labor shortages. For example, many Afghan refugees have backgrounds in construction and logistics, while Syrian refugees often excel in healthcare and education.

Di Tran Enterprise's Role:
Di Tran Enterprise acts as a matchmaker, aligning refugees' skills with industry needs. Through strategic partnerships with businesses, the organization identifies opportunities where refugees can immediately contribute while receiving on-the-job training to refine their skills further.

---

2. Cultural Wealth

Refugees enrich America's cultural tapestry, introducing traditions, cuisines, and perspectives that enhance community life. Their presence fosters greater understanding and appreciation of global diversity.

Di Tran Enterprise's Role:
To celebrate this cultural wealth, Di Tran Enterprise

organizes community events where refugees share their heritage through food, art, and storytelling. These events not only build bridges between refugees and their neighbors but also create opportunities for refugees to showcase their entrepreneurial talents, such as catering or handmade crafts.

---

3. Economic Potential

Empowered refugees are significant contributors to local economies. They start businesses, pay taxes, and fill critical roles in industries facing labor shortages. According to studies, refugees are more likely than native-born Americans to become entrepreneurs, creating jobs and driving economic growth.

Di Tran Enterprise's Role:
Di Tran Enterprise helps refugees transition from employees to employers. Through microloans, mentorship, and business training, the organization equips refugees to start and scale their businesses. This approach not only boosts local economies but also empowers refugees to become community leaders.

A Multi-Year Strategic Plan for Empowerment

To maximize the potential of refugees, Di Tran Enterprise proposes a multi-year strategy that integrates housing, employment, education, and community engagement. This blueprint serves as a model for government agencies seeking effective partnerships.

Year 1: Foundation Building

- **Housing First:** Establish affordable housing projects in regions with high refugee populations.

- **Language Immersion:** Launch intensive English training programs tailored to workforce needs.

- **Community Hubs:** Create centers where refugees can access resources, meet mentors, and build social connections.

Year 2: Workforce Development

Refugee Resilience:
Elevating Lives, Communities, and America

- **Skills Assessment:** Conduct comprehensive evaluations to match refugees' talents with industry demands.

- **Job Placement Programs:** Partner with businesses to provide apprenticeships and job opportunities.

- **Re-certification Support:** Work with licensing boards to streamline credential recognition for skilled refugees.

Year 3: Entrepreneurship and Leadership

- **Business Incubation:** Provide funding, mentorship, and training for refugee entrepreneurs.

- **Community Leadership Training:** Empower refugees to take active roles in local governance and advocacy.

- **Scaling Success:** Replicate successful programs in additional regions, ensuring broader impact.

Challenges and Opportunities for Government Collaboration

Government agencies often face challenges in implementing refugee programs effectively, including limited resources, bureaucratic hurdles, and cultural gaps. Di Tran Enterprise offers solutions that address these challenges while aligning with government goals.

Challenge 1: Resource Allocation

Government programs are often stretched thin, struggling to meet the needs of growing refugee populations.

Opportunity:
Di Tran Enterprise's hybrid model of private funding and public partnership ensures that resources are used efficiently, maximizing impact without overburdening government budgets.

Challenge 2: Cultural Gaps

Government agencies may lack the cultural competence needed to address refugees' unique needs effectively.

Refugee Resilience:
Elevating Lives, Communities, and America

Opportunity:

With its deep connections to refugee communities, Di Tran Enterprise provides culturally informed services that bridge these gaps, ensuring programs are both effective and respectful.

Challenge 3: Measuring Impact

Demonstrating the effectiveness of refugee programs is essential for securing ongoing funding and public support.

Opportunity:

Di Tran Enterprise employs data-driven strategies to track outcomes, from job placement rates to community integration metrics. These measurable results provide accountability and justify continued investment.

A Vision for the Future

Di Tran Enterprise envisions a future where every refugee in America has the tools and support needed to succeed. By combining the strengths of government programs with the innovation and agility of private enterprise, we can create a system that

Refugee Resilience:
Elevating Lives, Communities, and America

transforms refugees into long-term assets for this country.

At its core, this vision is about more than just meeting basic needs. It's about fostering a mindset of *"Yes I CAN"*—a belief that with the right support, every refugee can achieve their full potential. It's about celebrating America as the #1 country on earth, a land where dreams are not only possible but inevitable for those willing to work for them.

This is the promise of Di Tran Enterprise: to serve as a bridge, a blueprint, and a beacon for refugees and the communities that welcome them. Through love, resilience, and unwavering commitment, we can build a brighter future for refugees and for America, one step at a time.

Chapter 3: Di Tran Enterprise – A Refugee-Driven Vision for Empowerment

When addressing the complexities of refugee resettlement, few organizations embody the blend of compassion, innovation, and measurable outcomes like **Di Tran Enterprise**. Driven by a deep understanding of the refugee experience, this organization is uniquely positioned to serve as a model for empowerment and integration. With its holistic approach and proven track record, Di Tran Enterprise is not just meeting immediate needs—it is redefining how refugees transition into thriving contributors to American society.

This chapter explores how Di Tran Enterprise operates as a multi-faceted entity, its tailored programs for addressing key challenges, and its ability to bridge the gap between government support and community needs. Through practical solutions, strategic initiatives, and a focus on long-term impact, Di Tran Enterprise is leading the way in creating sustainable opportunities for refugees and underrepresented communities.

Refugee Resilience:
Elevating Lives, Communities, and America

A Holistic Approach to Refugee Empowerment

Di Tran Enterprise views every refugee as a potential catalyst for positive change. Its approach is built on three interconnected pillars: **stability, growth, and community engagement**. Stability ensures that refugees have their basic needs met; growth focuses on personal and professional development, and community engagement fosters meaningful connections that drive integration and belonging.

This structure allows the organization to address the multi-dimensional challenges refugees face, ensuring no individual is left behind. Unlike traditional models that treat resettlement as a temporary process, Di Tran Enterprise designs programs that consider long-term outcomes, from economic independence to community leadership.

Core Programs Designed for Impact

1. Comprehensive Workforce Development

For refugees, securing employment is often the first step toward self-reliance. However, barriers such as unrecognized skills, language limitations, and lack of professional networks can make this process daunting.

Di Tran Enterprise's Workforce Initiatives:

- **Targeted Training:** The organization develops industry-specific training modules for high-demand sectors such as construction, beauty, healthcare, and IT. These modules are tailored to align with current labor market needs, ensuring participants are job-ready upon completion.

- **Mentorship Integration:** Refugees are paired with mentors from similar professional backgrounds to provide guidance and networking opportunities.

- **Credential Recognition Support:** For skilled refugees, Di Tran Enterprise works with licensing boards and educational institutions to expedite the recognition of foreign certifications.

Through these efforts, participants not only secure employment but also embark on career trajectories that foster upward mobility.

Refugee Resilience:
Elevating Lives, Communities, and America

2. Affordable Housing Solutions

Stable housing is a cornerstone of successful resettlement. Refugees often face challenges such as limited income, lack of credit history, and rising rental costs in urban areas.

Innovative Housing Strategies:

- **Multi-Family Developments:** Di Tran Enterprise collaborates with local governments and investors to build affordable, energy-efficient housing complexes tailored for refugee families.

- **Transitional Housing Programs:** For newly arrived refugees, short-term housing solutions provide a safe and supportive environment while they acclimate to their new surroundings.

- **Pathways to Ownership:** Through financial literacy training and microloans, refugees are empowered to move from renters to homeowners, creating generational stability.

These initiatives not only address immediate housing needs but also create opportunities for long-term financial security.

3. Education and Skill-Building

Education is a transformative tool for refugees, providing the foundation for self-confidence and societal contribution. Di Tran Enterprise prioritizes learning opportunities that go beyond traditional academic settings, focusing instead on practical, actionable knowledge.

Programs Tailored to Refugees' Needs:

- **Language for Living:** English classes are integrated with everyday scenarios, from navigating healthcare appointments to participating in parent-teacher conferences.

- **Hands-On Training:** Refugees are trained in trades and skills that allow them to enter the workforce immediately, such as cosmetology through Louisville Beauty Academy.

- **Entrepreneurship Workshops:** Aspiring business owners receive training in business planning, customer service, and operations, giving them the tools to succeed as entrepreneurs.

Refugee Resilience:
Elevating Lives, Communities, and America

These educational programs ensure refugees can confidently navigate their new lives while building sustainable futures.

---

4. Community Integration Programs

Beyond housing and employment, true integration requires a sense of belonging. Many refugees experience isolation due to cultural and linguistic differences, which can hinder their ability to engage fully in their communities.

Fostering Connections:

- **Cultural Exchange Events:** Di Tran Enterprise organizes events where refugees and local residents share traditions, food, and stories, fostering mutual respect and understanding.

- **Volunteerism:** Refugees are encouraged to participate in community service, allowing them to give back and build connections with their neighbors.

- **Youth Leadership Programs:** Refugee children and teens are offered leadership training to help them excel in school and extracurricular activities, setting them up for future success.

By prioritizing inclusion, Di Tran Enterprise ensures that refugees become active, valued members of their communities.

Innovation and Adaptability: Keys to Success

Di Tran Enterprise stands apart due to its ability to innovate and adapt. The organization continuously refines its programs based on feedback, data, and evolving community needs. For instance, recognizing the rise of remote work, Di Tran Enterprise recently launched digital literacy training, ensuring refugees can compete in a technology-driven job market.

This forward-thinking approach allows the organization to remain relevant and effective, addressing not only current challenges but also anticipating future trends.

Why Di Tran Enterprise Is the Ideal Government Partner

Refugee Resilience:
Elevating Lives, Communities, and America

Government agencies play a vital role in refugee resettlement, but they often face limitations such as stretched resources, bureaucratic processes, and gaps in cultural understanding. Di Tran Enterprise offers solutions that complement government efforts, maximizing impact while minimizing inefficiencies.

1. Grassroots Expertise

With deep ties to refugee communities, Di Tran Enterprise provides culturally informed services that ensure programs resonate with participants. This grassroots connection builds trust and facilitates effective implementation.

2. Accountability and Measurable Outcomes

The organization operates with a data-driven mindset, tracking key metrics such as job placement rates, housing stability, and program satisfaction. These measurable outcomes demonstrate accountability and provide a clear return on investment for government partners.

3. Cost-Effective Models

By leveraging private funding and community resources, Di Tran Enterprise ensures that government contributions are used efficiently. This

Refugee Resilience:
Elevating Lives, Communities, and America

hybrid approach allows programs to scale without overburdening public budgets.

Multi-Year Strategy for Transformative Change

To create lasting impact, Di Tran Enterprise employs a multi-year strategy that aligns with both immediate needs and long-term goals.

Year 1: Establish Foundations

- Launch pilot programs in housing, workforce training, and community integration.

- Build partnerships with local governments, businesses, and community organizations.

- Establish data collection systems to measure impact and refine strategies.

Year 2: Expand Reach

- Scale successful pilot programs to additional regions.

- Develop specialized initiatives for vulnerable populations, such as single mothers and elderly refugees.

Refugee Resilience:
Elevating Lives, Communities, and America

- Introduce advanced training programs in emerging industries like renewable energy and digital technology.

Year 3: Foster Leadership and Independence

- Transition program graduates into leadership roles, creating peer mentorship opportunities.

- Expand entrepreneurial initiatives, supporting refugees in launching businesses that create jobs and stimulate local economies.

- Advocate for policy changes that streamline refugee integration processes, using data and success stories as evidence.

A Vision for the Future

Di Tran Enterprise envisions a future where refugees are not just survivors but thriving contributors to American society. By addressing challenges holistically and building on refugees' strengths, the organization creates pathways for multi-generational success.

Refugee Resilience:
Elevating Lives, Communities, and America

With its commitment to love, action, and innovation, Di Tran Enterprise is redefining what it means to empower refugees. This vision is not just aspirational—it is actionable, grounded in real programs, measurable results, and a proven track record.

As a bridge between policy and people, Di Tran Enterprise is the ideal partner for government agencies seeking sustainable, impactful solutions. Together, we can ensure that refugees are not only welcomed but empowered to build better lives—for themselves and for the communities they now call home.

Chapter 4: Building the Perfect Partnership with Government

Addressing the challenges of refugee resettlement requires collaboration, innovation, and a shared commitment to sustainable outcomes. While government agencies provide essential frameworks and funding, the true impact lies in how these resources are implemented at the community level. This is where organizations like **Di Tran Enterprise** step in—not as mere participants, but as strategic partners with the capacity to execute, innovate, and connect policy to practice.

Through a shared vision of empowerment and integration, Di Tran Enterprise complements government efforts by addressing gaps in service delivery, offering culturally informed programs, and creating measurable outcomes. This chapter outlines how Di Tran Enterprise bridges the divide between government policy and refugee communities, offering actionable strategies and multi-year plans for long-term impact.

The Value of Public-Private Collaboration

Public-private partnerships are not just a mechanism for resource allocation—they are transformative relationships that enhance both reach and efficiency. Governments establish the foundation through funding, policies, and oversight, while private organizations bring agility, local expertise, and innovative approaches.

1. Government's Role

- **Funding Allocation:** Governments provide the financial support necessary to sustain refugee programs, from housing subsidies to workforce grants.

- **Policy Direction:** Federal and state agencies set the guidelines that shape refugee resettlement and integration.

- **Data Resources:** Access to research and statistics helps guide evidence-based interventions.

2. Di Tran Enterprise's Contribution

- **Localized Execution:** By working directly with refugee communities, the organization ensures programs are adapted to specific needs and cultural nuances.

- **Innovative Solutions:** Di Tran Enterprise designs tailored initiatives, from hybrid housing models to skill-building programs aligned with industry demands.

- **Trust Building:** Acting as a cultural bridge, the organization fosters trust between refugees and service providers, enhancing participation and outcomes.

Programs That Deliver Impact

1. Workforce Integration

Gap Identified: While job opportunities exist, many refugees struggle to navigate the U.S. job market due to language barriers, limited networks, and a lack of familiarity with workplace norms.

Solution:

- **Sector-Specific Training:** Partnering with industries such as healthcare, technology, and skilled trades, Di Tran Enterprise develops customized training modules that

Refugee Resilience:
Elevating Lives, Communities, and America

combine technical skills with workplace readiness.

- **Employment Readiness Workshops:** These sessions cover resume building, interview preparation, and understanding workplace etiquette.

- **Employer Partnerships:** Collaborating with local businesses to match refugees with immediate job opportunities and long-term career pathways.

---

2. Holistic Housing Solutions

Gap Identified: Affordable housing for refugees remains scarce, with many families forced into substandard or overcrowded living conditions.

Solution:

- **Community-Based Housing Developments:** Affordable housing projects that incorporate shared spaces for community events and resources such as childcare and job centers.

Refugee Resilience:
Elevating Lives, Communities, and America

- **Financial Literacy Programs:** Educating refugees on budgeting, saving, and credit building to prepare them for homeownership.

- **Partnership Models:** Leveraging federal housing grants alongside private investment to scale housing initiatives sustainably.

---

3. Cultural Integration and Social Engagement

Gap Identified: Refugees often feel isolated in their new communities, which can hinder their ability to adapt and thrive.

Solution:

- **Community Liaisons:** Refugees are paired with local mentors who provide guidance on navigating cultural norms and community resources.

- **Intercultural Programs:** Events and workshops that bring together refugees and local residents to share traditions, fostering mutual respect and understanding.

- **Youth Leadership Initiatives:** Programs designed to empower refugee youth through education, extracurricular activities, and leadership training.

Accountability and Measurable Outcomes

Effectiveness is not measured by effort but by results. Di Tran Enterprise emphasizes transparency and accountability, ensuring every initiative is backed by measurable success metrics.

1. Data-Driven Insights

- **Employment Metrics:** Tracking job placements, salary growth, and career progression among program participants.

- **Housing Outcomes:** Monitoring transitions from rental assistance to homeownership over time.

- **Engagement Rates:** Measuring participation in mentorship, education, and community programs to assess impact.

2. Sustainability Models

- **Private Investment:** Leveraging partnerships with businesses and philanthropic organizations to diversify funding streams.

Refugee Resilience:
Elevating Lives, Communities, and America

- **Program Scalability:** Designing initiatives that can be replicated across different regions and contexts without compromising quality.

- **Participant Empowerment:** Training program graduates to become mentors, educators, or leaders within their own communities, ensuring long-term self-sufficiency.

Overcoming Challenges Through Partnership

1. Limited Funding Capacity

Government budgets are often stretched, limiting the reach and depth of refugee programs.

Collaborative Approach:
Di Tran Enterprise amplifies government funding by combining it with private resources, ensuring programs are both robust and scalable.

---

2. Cultural Disconnects

Standardized approaches can overlook the specific needs and experiences of diverse refugee groups.

Refugee Resilience:
Elevating Lives, Communities, and America

Collaborative Approach:
With its deep cultural understanding and community ties, Di Tran Enterprise adapts programs to reflect the unique backgrounds and traditions of refugee populations.

---

3. Bureaucratic Inefficiencies

Complex administrative processes can delay the implementation of critical services.

Collaborative Approach:
As a nimble, community-focused organization, Di Tran Enterprise works to streamline processes, reducing delays and ensuring timely delivery of resources.

A Multi-Year Roadmap for Success

To ensure lasting impact, Di Tran Enterprise proposes a multi-year strategy that integrates government priorities with on-the-ground execution.

Year 1: Pilot and Refine

Refugee Resilience:
Elevating Lives, Communities, and America

- **Program Launches:** Initiate pilot projects in key regions, focusing on housing, workforce development, and cultural integration.

- **Stakeholder Engagement:** Build relationships with local governments, businesses, and refugee advocacy groups.

- **Impact Measurement:** Develop baseline metrics to evaluate program effectiveness.

Year 2: Scale and Innovate

- **Regional Expansion:** Extend successful pilot programs to additional states and municipalities.

- **Technology Integration:** Leverage digital platforms for language training, mentorship, and employment matching.

- **Targeted Interventions:** Develop specialized programs for underserved groups, such as single mothers, seniors, or disabled refugees.

Year 3: Institutionalize and Lead

- **Leadership Development:** Transition program alumni into mentorship and leadership roles within their communities.

- **Policy Advocacy:** Use data and success stories to advocate for reforms that simplify refugee integration.

- **Blueprint Creation:** Document best practices and create a replicable model for national and international adoption.

Why Di Tran Enterprise Stands Out

Di Tran Enterprise offers a unique combination of grassroots expertise, innovative program design, and unwavering accountability. By aligning its efforts with government priorities, the organization creates a synergy that multiplies the impact of refugee resettlement programs.

What sets Di Tran Enterprise apart is its focus on sustainable, long-term outcomes. Refugees supported by the organization do not merely adapt—they excel, becoming valued contributors to their communities and the broader economy. This success is a testament to the organization's core belief in empowerment, resilience, and the transformative power of opportunity.

A Vision for Collaborative Leadership

The future of refugee resettlement depends on partnerships that prioritize action, compassion, and results. Di Tran Enterprise envisions a world where public-private collaboration creates systems that empower refugees while strengthening American communities. By working together, we can build a nation where every refugee is not only welcomed but equipped to thrive.

This chapter presents Di Tran Enterprise as a strategic partner capable of transforming policy into practice, funding into opportunity, and hope into tangible success. With a clear vision and a proven roadmap, the organization is poised to lead the way in creating lasting, meaningful change.

Chapter 5: Housing Refugees – A Home for Every New Beginning

Housing is more than just a roof over one's head—it is the cornerstone of stability, security, and opportunity. For refugees arriving in the United States, finding affordable, safe housing is one of the most urgent challenges. Without a stable home, pursuing employment, education, and integration becomes significantly harder. This chapter delves into the critical role of housing in refugee resettlement, presenting **Di Tran Enterprise** as a transformative force in developing innovative, sustainable solutions that meet the needs of refugee communities while leveraging the strengths of public-private partnerships.

Di Tran Enterprise is uniquely positioned to address the housing challenges faced by refugees, combining deep expertise in real estate development with a commitment to community empowerment. By creating scalable housing models that integrate government funding with private investment, the organization provides a blueprint for addressing the housing crisis while setting refugees on a path to long-term success.

The Housing Crisis: Refugee Challenges and Barriers

For newly arrived refugees, the search for housing is often fraught with obstacles that extend beyond affordability. The complexities of navigating a new housing market, coupled with limited financial resources, exacerbate the challenges refugees face. Key issues include:

1. Affordability

Refugees often arrive with limited savings, no credit history, and minimal income, making it nearly impossible to compete in high-cost rental markets. Even with federal housing assistance, the demand for affordable units far exceeds supply.

2. Quality of Housing

When affordability is prioritized, quality often suffers. Refugees may end up in substandard housing, with overcrowded conditions, unsafe neighborhoods, or deteriorating infrastructure that affects their well-being.

3. Lack of Accessibility

Many refugees require housing near essential services such as schools, public transportation, healthcare facilities, and job opportunities. Yet, affordable housing in these areas is often scarce or inaccessible.

4. Discrimination and Bureaucracy

Refugees frequently face discrimination from landlords unwilling to rent to individuals with no credit history or steady income. In addition, navigating the administrative requirements for housing assistance can be daunting for those unfamiliar with U.S. systems or English.

Di Tran Enterprise: A Visionary Approach to Refugee Housing

Recognizing the central role housing plays in refugee resettlement, Di Tran Enterprise has made affordable housing a core pillar of its mission. With extensive experience in real estate development and a deep understanding of refugee needs, the organization designs and executes housing solutions that go beyond simply providing shelter.

---

1. Developing Scalable, Affordable Housing Models

Di Tran Enterprise leverages its expertise in real estate to create innovative housing projects that meet the unique needs of refugees. These developments are designed with sustainability, community, and scalability in mind.

Key Features of Housing Projects:

- **Mixed-Use Communities:** Developments include residential units alongside community spaces, childcare centers, and training facilities, creating self-sufficient hubs.

- **Energy-Efficient Designs:** Incorporating green technology reduces utility costs for tenants and aligns with broader sustainability goals.

- **Flexible Unit Sizes:** Housing units are designed to accommodate both individuals and large families, addressing the diverse needs of refugees.

Case Example:
In partnership with local governments, Di Tran

Refugee Resilience:
Elevating Lives, Communities, and America

Enterprise recently completed a 50-unit housing project tailored for refugee families. Each unit includes modern amenities and proximity to schools, transit lines, and job centers. The development also features a community center offering language classes, financial literacy workshops, and childcare services, ensuring families have the resources to thrive.

---

2. Public-Private Investment Models

Di Tran Enterprise understands that the scale of the housing crisis cannot be addressed through government funding alone. By combining public resources with private investment, the organization creates sustainable financing models that multiply impact while reducing the burden on taxpayers.

Financing Strategies:

- **Tax Credits for Investors:** Incentivizing private developers to participate in affordable housing projects through tax benefits.

- **Long-Term Lease Agreements:** Collaborating with government agencies to ensure affordability over extended periods.

Refugee Resilience:
Elevating Lives, Communities, and America

- **Community Investment Programs:** Encouraging local businesses and residents to invest in refugee housing as a means of fostering inclusive growth.

---

3. Pathways to Homeownership

Beyond rental housing, Di Tran Enterprise aims to empower refugees to achieve homeownership, creating long-term stability and generational wealth.

Programs Supporting Ownership:

- **Microloan Initiatives:** Providing refugees with low-interest loans for down payments on homes.

- **Financial Literacy Education:** Offering workshops on budgeting, saving, and understanding mortgages to prepare refugees for the responsibilities of homeownership.

- **Partnerships with Credit Unions:** Establishing relationships with financial institutions that support first-time buyers, particularly those with non-traditional credit histories.

Refugee Resilience:
Elevating Lives, Communities, and America

Impact:

In a recent initiative, 10 refugee families transitioned from rental housing to homeownership within three years. These families not only gained financial independence but also became active contributors to their neighborhoods, fostering stronger communities.

Why Housing Is the Foundation for Refugee Success

A stable home provides more than just physical security—it is the launching pad for every other aspect of refugee integration.

1. Enabling Economic Participation

With stable housing, refugees can focus on finding employment, attending training programs, and building careers. The stress of unstable living arrangements is removed, allowing them to fully engage in economic activities.

2. Supporting Educational Attainment

Children from refugee families benefit immensely from stable housing. Consistency in school attendance and access to safe study environments are critical for their academic success and future opportunities.

3. Strengthening Community Ties

Permanent, quality housing fosters a sense of belonging. Refugees are more likely to engage with their neighbors, participate in local events, and contribute to the social fabric of their communities when they feel secure in their living arrangements.

Challenges and Opportunities in Scaling Housing Solutions

While the need for affordable housing is urgent, addressing it at scale requires overcoming significant obstacles. Di Tran Enterprise is uniquely equipped to tackle these challenges while unlocking new opportunities.

Challenge 1: High Construction Costs

Building affordable housing is often financially prohibitive due to rising material and labor costs.

Opportunity:
By using modular construction techniques and sourcing sustainable materials, Di Tran Enterprise reduces costs without compromising quality.

Partnerships with vocational training programs also provide opportunities for refugees to contribute to construction, reducing labor expenses while gaining valuable skills.

Challenge 2: Limited Land Availability

Urban areas with the greatest need for affordable housing often face land shortages.

Opportunity:

Di Tran Enterprise identifies underutilized spaces, such as vacant lots and repurposed commercial buildings, to develop housing projects in high-demand areas.

Challenge 3: Balancing Affordability with Profitability

Private investors may be hesitant to fund projects perceived as low-return.

Opportunity:

By demonstrating the long-term social and economic benefits of affordable housing, Di Tran Enterprise attracts impact-driven investors who value both financial returns and community impact.

Refugee Resilience:
Elevating Lives, Communities, and America

A Multi-Year Strategy for Transformative Impact

Di Tran Enterprise employs a multi-year strategy to ensure sustainable, scalable housing solutions for refugees.

Year 1: Pilot Initiatives

- Launch small-scale housing projects to test innovative designs and financing models.

- Partner with local governments to identify priority areas and establish funding agreements.

- Build community advisory boards to ensure housing developments align with refugee needs.

Year 2: Regional Expansion

- Scale successful pilot projects to additional regions, focusing on areas with high refugee populations.

- Introduce programs supporting refugee homeownership, including microloans and financial counseling.

- Collaborate with workforce training programs to integrate refugees into construction and property management roles.

Year 3: National Integration

- Establish partnerships with federal agencies to replicate housing models nationwide.

- Advocate for policy changes that streamline affordable housing development and incentivize private investment.

- Create a comprehensive toolkit for other organizations to adopt Di Tran Enterprise's housing strategies.

Building a Legacy of Opportunity

Housing is not just a solution for today's challenges—it is an investment in tomorrow's potential. By providing refugees with stable, affordable homes, Di Tran Enterprise lays the groundwork for economic mobility, educational success, and community cohesion.

Refugee Resilience:
Elevating Lives, Communities, and America

This legacy extends far beyond the individuals served. Refugee housing developments become vibrant neighborhoods where diversity thrives, businesses flourish, and multi-generational success stories are written. Di Tran Enterprise's approach to housing is not merely about meeting immediate needs; it is about creating a foundation upon which refugees—and America as a whole—can build a brighter future.

As the nation continues to welcome refugees seeking safety and opportunity, Di Tran Enterprise offers a proven model for transforming housing challenges into lasting solutions. Through innovation, collaboration, and an unwavering belief in the potential of every individual, we ensure that every refugee has a place to call home—and a future to look forward to.

Chapter 6: Workforce Development – From Survival to Thriving

For refugees arriving in the United States, employment is not just a pathway to survival—it is a gateway to dignity, stability, and opportunity. A job offers more than an income; it provides a sense of purpose, belonging, and the chance to contribute to the community. Yet, navigating the complexities of the American workforce can be overwhelming for refugees facing language barriers, unrecognized credentials, and unfamiliar systems.

Di Tran Enterprise approaches workforce development with a clear mission: to transform refugees from job seekers into valued contributors and, ultimately, leaders in their chosen fields. By addressing the unique challenges refugees face, creating innovative training programs, and forging strategic partnerships with businesses, Di Tran Enterprise has built a model that not only empowers individuals but also strengthens the broader economy.

Refugee Resilience:
Elevating Lives, Communities, and America

Challenges Refugees Face in Workforce Integration

Refugees bring resilience, skills, and determination, but the journey to gainful employment is fraught with obstacles:

1. Language Barriers

For many refugees, limited proficiency in English is the most immediate challenge. Without strong communication skills, navigating job interviews, understanding workplace expectations, and connecting with colleagues becomes difficult.

2. Unrecognized Skills and Credentials

Refugees often arrive with valuable skills and professional experience from their home countries. However, the lack of recognition for foreign certifications or qualifications prevents them from working in their trained fields.

3. Cultural Adjustments

Differences in workplace norms and cultural expectations can make integration into the American workforce intimidating. Refugees may feel uncertain about unwritten rules regarding professional behavior, time management, and teamwork.

4. Limited Job Networks

Unlike native-born workers, refugees rarely have established networks to help them find job opportunities. This isolation further delays their ability to secure meaningful employment.

Di Tran Enterprise: A Holistic Workforce Development Model

Understanding these challenges, Di Tran Enterprise has crafted a multi-faceted approach that combines training, mentorship, and partnerships to create a seamless transition from survival to thriving.

1. Language Training for Workplace Success

Language is the foundation for workforce integration, and Di Tran Enterprise integrates English instruction into every aspect of its workforce development programs.

Key Features of Language Programs:

- **Job-Oriented English Courses:** Classes focus on practical vocabulary and communication skills tailored to specific industries, such as healthcare, construction, and retail.

- **Immersive Training:** Participants practice English in simulated workplace scenarios, such as mock interviews, team meetings, and customer interactions.

- **Bilingual Mentorship:** Refugees are paired with bilingual mentors who provide one-on-one support, helping them build confidence in real-world situations.

Outcome:
Graduates of these programs consistently demonstrate improved communication skills, enabling them to secure jobs and build stronger connections with colleagues and clients.

---

2. Skill Recognition and Certification Pathways

To bridge the gap between refugees' existing expertise and American workforce requirements, Di Tran Enterprise offers pathways for skill recognition and certification.

Programs for Credential Alignment:

Refugee Resilience:
Elevating Lives, Communities, and America

- **Fast-Track Re-Certification:** Collaborations with licensing boards to expedite the validation of foreign credentials for professions such as nursing, engineering, and teaching.

- **Skill Evaluation Workshops:** Refugees undergo assessments to identify transferable skills and potential career pathways.

- **Training for Licensing Exams:** Targeted preparation courses help participants pass state and national certification exams.

Success Story:
A Syrian refugee with a background in dentistry was able to resume her career in the U.S. after completing a re-certification program through Di Tran Enterprise, allowing her to practice in a high-demand area and fill a critical healthcare gap.

---

3. Strategic Partnerships with Local Businesses

Employment is more than an outcome—it is a collaborative effort between refugees, training organizations, and employers. Di Tran Enterprise works closely with local businesses to connect

Refugee Resilience:
Elevating Lives, Communities, and America

refugees with job opportunities that align with their skills and interests.

Employer Collaboration Initiatives:

- **Workplace Integration Programs:** Employers receive cultural competency training to better support refugee employees, ensuring mutual success.

- **Apprenticeships and Internships:** Refugees gain hands-on experience through structured programs, often leading to permanent employment.

- **Customized Hiring Pipelines:** Di Tran Enterprise designs tailored hiring programs for businesses, matching refugees to specific roles based on their skills.

Impact:
Through partnerships with over 50 businesses, Di Tran Enterprise has placed more than 1,000 refugees in stable jobs across industries, including manufacturing, hospitality, and healthcare.

---

4. Entrepreneurial Programs to Build Refugee-Owned Businesses

Refugee Resilience:
Elevating Lives, Communities, and America

For many refugees, entrepreneurship represents not just an opportunity to earn a livelihood but also a chance to reclaim their independence and create lasting value in their communities.

Support for Aspiring Entrepreneurs:

- **Business Development Workshops:** Refugees learn the fundamentals of starting and running a business, including marketing, operations, and financial management.

- **Microloan Access:** Di Tran Enterprise connects entrepreneurs with low-interest loans to cover startup costs, such as equipment and inventory.

- **Co-Working Spaces:** Refugee entrepreneurs gain access to affordable workspaces where they can collaborate and grow their businesses.

Success Story:
Inspired by his own entrepreneurial journey, Di Tran worked with a Congolese refugee to establish a catering business specializing in African cuisine. Today, the business employs five other refugees and has become a beloved staple in its community.

Refugee Resilience:
Elevating Lives, Communities, and America

Sector-Specific Initiatives: Beauty, Pharmacy, and More

Di Tran Enterprise tailors its programs to meet the unique demands of specific industries, ensuring refugees are prepared to succeed in high-demand fields.

1. Beauty Industry Training

- **Programs Offered:** Refugees are trained in cosmetology, nail care, and esthetics through Louisville Beauty Academy, gaining the certifications needed to work in salons or start their own businesses.

- **Cultural Integration:** Participants learn customer service skills and beauty trends specific to American markets, enhancing their employability.

- **Results:** Hundreds of program graduates now work as licensed beauty professionals, many of whom have opened their own salons.

2. Pharmacy and Healthcare

- **Programs Offered:** Refugees with healthcare backgrounds are provided fast-track training to enter roles as pharmacy technicians, nursing assistants, and lab technicians.

- **Collaboration with Employers:** Di Tran Enterprise works with hospitals and pharmacies to create internship opportunities for trainees.

- **Results:** Graduates fill critical roles in underserved areas, addressing workforce shortages while advancing their own careers.

3. Emerging Sectors

- **Technology Training:** Refugees are trained in IT support, coding, and data entry, equipping them for remote and in-office roles in the digital economy.

- **Sustainability Careers:** Di Tran Enterprise has launched programs in renewable energy and green construction, preparing refugees for careers in these growing sectors.

Addressing Challenges in Workforce Development

Refugee Resilience:
Elevating Lives, Communities, and America

While the successes are many, integrating refugees into the workforce requires ongoing innovation and problem-solving.

Challenge 1: Matching Skills to Market Needs

Refugees often possess skills that do not align directly with local job markets.

Solution:

Di Tran Enterprise conducts market analyses to identify industries with labor shortages, then designs training programs to prepare refugees for these roles.

Challenge 2: Navigating Bureaucracy

The process of obtaining work authorization and certifications can be lengthy and complex.

Solution:

Di Tran Enterprise provides case management services, helping refugees navigate paperwork and connect with legal and administrative support.

Challenge 3: Balancing Immediate Employment with Long-Term Growth

Refugee Resilience:
Elevating Lives, Communities, and America

While some refugees prioritize immediate income, others seek career advancement opportunities.

Solution:
Programs are structured to offer flexibility, allowing refugees to start with entry-level roles while pursuing additional training for higher-level positions.

A Multi-Year Strategy for Workforce Transformation

Di Tran Enterprise's approach to workforce development is guided by a strategic vision that ensures sustainable, scalable impact.

Year 1: Laying the Groundwork

- Launch pilot training programs in key industries.

- Build partnerships with local businesses and workforce boards.

- Establish mentorship networks to support participants throughout their career journeys.

Year 2: Scaling Up

Refugee Resilience:
Elevating Lives, Communities, and America

- Expand training programs to additional regions.

- Introduce specialized initiatives for refugee women, youth, and seniors.

- Collaborate with universities and trade schools to offer advanced certifications.

Year 3: Creating Leaders

- Transition program graduates into mentorship and leadership roles.

- Support refugee-owned businesses in scaling and hiring additional employees.

- Advocate for policies that simplify credential recognition and workforce integration.

The Bigger Picture: Refugees as Drivers of Economic Growth

Refugees are not just beneficiaries of workforce development—they are contributors to economic growth, innovation, and community resilience. Di Tran Enterprise's programs demonstrate how

Refugee Resilience:
Elevating Lives, Communities, and America

empowering refugees benefits not only individuals but also local economies and industries.

By focusing on language, skills, partnerships, and entrepreneurship, Di Tran Enterprise has created a model that turns challenges into opportunities and aspirations into achievements. Through its results-oriented approach and unwavering commitment to *"Yes I CAN"*, the organization sets a new standard for workforce development—one that ensures every refugee has the chance to thrive and contribute to the greatest country on earth.

Chapter 7: Education and Training – Empowering the Next Generation

Education is a transformative tool that opens doors to opportunity, independence, and lasting success. For refugees arriving in the United States, education is more than a means of learning—it is the bridge between survival and thriving. Refugees and their families often face significant barriers to accessing quality education and training, but these obstacles can be overcome with the right support, resources, and programs tailored to their unique needs.

Di Tran Enterprise is committed to ensuring that education serves as a launchpad for refugees, empowering them to contribute meaningfully to the communities they join. Through a combination of innovative programs, mentorship, and real-world application, Di Tran Enterprise offers a blueprint for equipping refugees with the knowledge and skills necessary to succeed in the American workforce and beyond.

The Role of Education in Refugee Success

Refugee Resilience:
Elevating Lives, Communities, and America

Education provides refugees with the tools to rebuild their lives, adapt to new environments, and achieve long-term stability. Its impact is multifaceted, influencing economic independence, social integration, and personal growth.

1. Economic Independence

Access to education allows refugees to gain the skills and credentials needed to secure well-paying jobs. Training in high-demand fields ensures that refugees not only meet immediate needs but also build sustainable careers.

2. Social Integration

Education fosters understanding and engagement, helping refugees navigate cultural norms, communicate effectively, and build connections within their communities.

3. Empowerment of Future Generations

For refugee children, education is the key to breaking cycles of poverty and creating multi-generational success. Parents who prioritize education set a strong foundation for their children's future achievements.

Refugee Resilience:
Elevating Lives, Communities, and America

Barriers to Refugee Education

Despite its importance, education remains one of the most significant challenges for refugees. Key obstacles include:

1. Language Limitations

Limited proficiency in English creates a barrier to accessing educational programs, understanding coursework, and participating fully in training opportunities.

2. Financial Constraints

Many refugees prioritize basic needs such as housing and food, leaving little room to invest in education or training programs.

3. Cultural Differences

Differences in teaching styles, educational expectations, and institutional norms can make it difficult for refugees to adjust to American education systems.

4. Lack of Accessibility

Geographic, technological, and transportation barriers often limit refugees' ability to attend classes or access online learning platforms.

Di Tran Enterprise: Revolutionizing Refugee Education

Di Tran Enterprise addresses these challenges with innovative programs that blend traditional education, hands-on training, and mentorship. The organization's education initiatives are designed to remove barriers, build confidence, and provide refugees with practical skills for real-world application.

1. Programs at Louisville Beauty Academy

One of the flagship initiatives of Di Tran Enterprise is **Louisville Beauty Academy**, which serves as a model for how education can be tailored to meet the needs of refugees and immigrants.

Key Features:

- **Affordable Training:** The academy provides low-cost programs in cosmetology, nail care, and esthetics, ensuring accessibility for those with limited financial resources.

- **Hands-On Learning:** Students gain practical experience through supervised training, allowing them to build confidence and refine their skills in a real-world setting.

- **Licensure Preparation:** Graduates are equipped with the certifications needed to enter the workforce immediately upon completing their programs.

Impact:

Hundreds of graduates from Louisville Beauty Academy have gone on to secure employment, start their own businesses, and contribute to their communities, demonstrating how targeted education can drive economic mobility.

---

2. Specialized Training Programs

Recognizing the diverse needs of refugee populations, Di Tran Enterprise has developed training programs across multiple industries, ensuring participants can pursue careers aligned with their skills and interests.

Healthcare Training:

- Programs in nursing assistance, pharmacy technology, and healthcare administration prepare refugees to fill critical roles in the medical field.

- Partnerships with hospitals and clinics provide internship opportunities, enabling hands-on experience and direct pathways to employment.

Technical Fields:

- Refugees are trained in IT support, coding, and data analytics, equipping them for roles in the rapidly growing tech industry.

- Courses include digital literacy, enabling participants to navigate online platforms and modern workplace tools.

Education Sector:

- For refugees with teaching backgrounds, Di Tran Enterprise offers pathways to re-certification and placement in local schools, where their multilingual skills and cultural perspectives are invaluable.

---

3. Real-World Application Through Mentorship

Refugee Resilience:
Elevating Lives, Communities, and America

Education at Di Tran Enterprise extends beyond the classroom. Mentorship is a cornerstone of every program, ensuring that participants receive guidance and support as they transition into new roles.

Mentorship Initiatives:

- **Industry-Specific Guidance:** Refugees are paired with mentors who have experience in their chosen fields, providing insights into industry norms and expectations.

- **Leadership Development:** Participants are encouraged to take on leadership roles within their training programs, building confidence and fostering independence.

- **Peer Support Networks:** Alumni of Di Tran Enterprise programs often return as mentors, creating a cycle of support and empowerment.

Leveraging Government Grants for Educational Impact

Di Tran Enterprise collaborates with government agencies to secure funding for its educational programs, ensuring scalability and sustainability. By aligning initiatives with federal and state priorities, the organization maximizes the impact of government investments.

Grant-Funded Programs:

- **Workforce Development Grants:** Support training in high-demand fields such as healthcare and technology, addressing labor shortages while empowering refugees.

- **Language Education Grants:** Fund English-language programs that integrate cultural orientation and workplace readiness.

- **Community College Partnerships:** Grants support collaborations with local colleges to provide refugees with access to degree programs and vocational training.

Challenges in Scaling Refugee Education

While Di Tran Enterprise has achieved significant success, scaling its educational programs to meet growing demand requires addressing ongoing challenges.

1. Expanding Reach

Refugee Resilience:
Elevating Lives, Communities, and America

Limited infrastructure and staffing capacity can make it difficult to serve all refugees in need.

Solution:
Di Tran Enterprise is investing in digital learning platforms that allow participants to access coursework remotely, increasing flexibility and reach.

---

2. Ensuring Long-Term Funding

Educational programs often rely on short-term grants, creating uncertainty for future initiatives.

Solution:
The organization is building partnerships with private donors and corporate sponsors to diversify funding streams and ensure long-term stability.

---

3. Adapting to Diverse Needs

Refugees come from varied backgrounds, requiring programs to be flexible and culturally responsive.

Solution:
Di Tran Enterprise conducts needs assessments within refugee communities, tailoring programs to reflect participants' unique experiences and goals.

Refugee Resilience:
Elevating Lives, Communities, and America

A Multi-Year Strategy for Refugee Education

To expand its impact, Di Tran Enterprise has developed a multi-year strategy for scaling its educational programs and creating lasting change.

Year 1: Building Foundations

- Launch pilot programs in underserved regions, focusing on healthcare, technology, and education training.

- Establish mentorship networks to support program participants.

- Create partnerships with local colleges and training institutes to expand access to advanced certifications.

Year 2: Scaling Impact

- Develop online learning platforms to increase accessibility for remote and rural refugees.

- Expand programs to include specialized tracks for women, youth, and seniors.

Refugee Resilience:
Elevating Lives, Communities, and America

- Introduce advanced technical training in emerging industries such as renewable energy and artificial intelligence.

Year 3: Creating Leaders

- Transition program graduates into roles as mentors, trainers, and community advocates.

- Launch entrepreneurship-focused programs that empower refugees to start businesses in their trained fields.

- Advocate for policy reforms that support refugee access to education and training at all levels.

Education as a Pathway to Independence

The impact of education extends far beyond individual success. Refugees who gain access to quality training and mentorship become role models within their communities, inspiring others to pursue their own goals. By investing in education, Di Tran Enterprise ensures that refugees are not just surviving but thriving, contributing to their families, their communities, and the nation.

Refugee Resilience:
Elevating Lives, Communities, and America

Through its innovative programs, targeted initiatives, and strategic partnerships, Di Tran Enterprise is redefining refugee education. With a focus on practical outcomes and long-term empowerment, the organization is creating pathways to independence that will serve refugees—and the United States—for generations to come.

Education is not just a tool; it is a promise. At Di Tran Enterprise, this promise is fulfilled every day, one student at a time.

Chapter 8: Refugee Mental Health and Community Integration

The journey of a refugee is one of profound resilience, but it is often accompanied by deep emotional and psychological scars. Fleeing war, persecution, or economic hardship, many refugees arrive in the United States with unaddressed trauma, compounded by the stress of adapting to a new country. The challenges of isolation, culture shock, and language barriers can further exacerbate feelings of displacement, impacting mental health and hindering the integration process.

Di Tran Enterprise understands that successful resettlement is not just about meeting physical needs—it is about addressing the emotional and social dimensions of integration. By creating programs that prioritize mental health and foster community connections, the organization provides a blueprint for ensuring that refugees not only survive but thrive in their new environment.

This chapter explores the mental health challenges refugees face, the importance of cultural integration, and the role Di Tran Enterprise plays in creating a

Refugee Resilience:
Elevating Lives, Communities, and America

supportive ecosystem that bridges the gap between policy and people.

The Mental Health Challenges Refugees Face

1. Trauma from Past Experiences

Refugees often carry the weight of traumatic experiences, such as violence, loss, or forced displacement. These experiences can lead to conditions such as post-traumatic stress disorder (PTSD), anxiety, and depression, which may go unrecognized or untreated.

2. Stress of Adapting to a New Culture

Adjusting to a new language, social norms, and legal systems can create overwhelming stress for refugees, particularly those without support networks. This stress can manifest in emotional exhaustion and feelings of inadequacy.

3. Isolation and Loneliness

The separation from family, friends, and familiar environments can leave refugees feeling isolated. This lack of social connection often contributes to poor mental health outcomes, especially for those living in areas without established refugee communities.

4. Stigma Around Mental Health

In many cultures, mental health issues are stigmatized, discouraging refugees from seeking help. This can lead to untreated conditions that impede personal and professional growth.

Di Tran Enterprise: A Holistic Approach to Mental Health and Integration

Recognizing the critical role mental health plays in overall well-being, Di Tran Enterprise integrates mental health support into its broader resettlement and workforce development programs. These initiatives are designed to address emotional challenges while fostering a sense of belonging and purpose.

---

1. Counseling Services Tailored to Refugees

Providing access to culturally competent mental health services is a cornerstone of Di Tran Enterprise's approach.

Refugee Resilience:
Elevating Lives, Communities, and America

Key Features:

- **Trauma-Informed Therapy:** Licensed counselors trained in trauma-specific care help refugees process past experiences and develop coping strategies.

- **Multilingual Support:** Services are offered in multiple languages, ensuring refugees can communicate their needs without language barriers.

- **Family Counseling:** Programs address the unique dynamics within refugee families, helping parents and children navigate cultural differences and shared challenges.

Impact:

Refugees who participate in counseling programs report improved emotional well-being, greater confidence, and enhanced ability to focus on education, employment, and personal goals.

---

2. Peer Support Groups

Sharing experiences with others who have faced similar challenges can be incredibly therapeutic for refugees. Di Tran Enterprise facilitates peer support groups that provide both emotional connection and practical guidance.

How It Works:

- **Community Circles:** Refugees meet regularly in facilitated groups to discuss common challenges, share resources, and support one another.

- **Mentorship Programs:** Refugees who have successfully navigated the integration process serve as mentors, offering encouragement and advice to newcomers.

- **Specialized Groups:** Focused support is provided for women, youth, and seniors, addressing their specific needs and concerns.

Success Story:
A Congolese refugee who struggled with isolation found a support network through Di Tran Enterprise's peer group for single mothers. Today, she not only leads a thriving life but also mentors other women in similar situations.

3. Cultural Integration Programs

Refugee Resilience:
Elevating Lives, Communities, and America

Understanding and embracing American culture is an essential step for refugees, but it doesn't mean abandoning their own traditions. Di Tran Enterprise creates programs that celebrate cultural diversity while fostering understanding and connection.

Integration Initiatives:

- **Cultural Orientation Workshops:** Refugees learn about American social norms, legal systems, and community resources through interactive sessions.

- **Celebration of Heritage:** Events such as cultural festivals and food fairs allow refugees to share their traditions with the broader community, building mutual respect and appreciation.

- **Civic Engagement Training:** Programs encourage refugees to participate in local governance, volunteerism, and community activities, empowering them to become active citizens.

Impact:

These initiatives create bridges between refugees and their new communities, reducing feelings of alienation and fostering a sense of pride in their dual identities.

---

4. Building Local Partnerships for Community Integration

Community integration is most successful when it involves collaboration across multiple sectors. Di Tran Enterprise works with local governments, schools, religious organizations, and non-profits to create a robust network of support for refugees.

Collaborative Efforts:

- **Partnerships with Religious Organizations:** Churches, mosques, and temples provide safe spaces for refugees to connect with others who share their faith and values.

- **Schools as Integration Hubs:** Collaborations with local schools ensure that refugee children receive emotional support while their parents engage in educational workshops.

- **Volunteer Programs:** Refugees are paired with local volunteers who help them navigate daily life, from grocery shopping to job interviews.

Example:

In Louisville, a partnership with a local church allowed Di Tran Enterprise to host weekly community dinners, where refugees and residents could bond over shared meals. These events have led to lasting friendships and greater understanding between diverse groups.

Addressing Challenges in Mental Health and Integration

While the initiatives outlined above are impactful, certain challenges require ongoing attention to ensure that mental health and integration programs remain effective and inclusive.

1. Overcoming Stigma

In many cultures, mental health issues are not openly discussed, leading to reluctance in seeking help.

Solution:

Di Tran Enterprise normalizes mental health care through public awareness campaigns, testimonials from program participants, and integration of counseling into everyday activities, such as language classes or job training.

2. Reaching Underserved Populations

Refugees in rural or underserved areas often lack access to mental health services and community programs.

Solution:

Mobile outreach teams bring services directly to these communities, while virtual counseling options increase accessibility for those in remote locations.

3. Sustaining Community Engagement

Maintaining engagement in integration programs can be challenging as refugees balance competing priorities.

Solution:

Programs are designed to be flexible and inclusive, with activities scheduled at convenient times and locations. Childcare services are also provided to remove barriers to participation.

Refugee Resilience:
Elevating Lives, Communities, and America

A Multi-Year Strategy for Refugee Mental Health and Integration

To create lasting impact, Di Tran Enterprise employs a phased approach to expanding its mental health and integration programs.

Year 1: Establishing Core Services

- Launch trauma-informed counseling and peer support groups in high-need areas.

- Build partnerships with local organizations to create cultural orientation workshops.

- Pilot community events that celebrate refugee heritage while fostering connections with residents.

Year 2: Expanding Reach and Impact

- Introduce mobile counseling units and virtual support options to serve rural and remote communities.

- Develop specialized programs for at-risk groups, such as unaccompanied minors and elderly refugees.

- Train community leaders and volunteers in cultural competency to enhance integration efforts.

Year 3: Building Self-Sustaining Communities

- Transition program participants into leadership roles as peer mentors, community advocates, and program facilitators.

- Expand civic engagement initiatives to include voter education and advocacy training.

- Collaborate with policymakers to incorporate mental health and integration support into broader refugee resettlement frameworks.

Fostering a Culture of Belonging

The success of refugee resettlement depends not only on meeting basic needs but also on creating an environment where refugees feel valued and connected. By addressing mental health challenges and building bridges between cultures, Di Tran Enterprise ensures that refugees are not just

Refugee Resilience:
Elevating Lives, Communities, and America

surviving but thriving as active members of their communities.

Through innovative programs, strategic partnerships, and a deep commitment to inclusion, Di Tran Enterprise is redefining what it means to welcome refugees. The organization's holistic approach demonstrates that mental health and community integration are not separate from economic success—they are its foundation.

As refugees heal, connect, and grow, they enrich the communities they join, creating a legacy of resilience, diversity, and shared prosperity. At the heart of this transformation is Di Tran Enterprise, setting the standard for compassionate, results-oriented refugee support in the United States.

Chapter 9: Why America is the Greatest Country on Earth

There is no greater symbol of hope, freedom, and opportunity than the United States of America. For centuries, America has been a sanctuary for those fleeing persecution, poverty, and violence, offering a chance to rebuild lives and achieve dreams that once seemed impossible. Refugees from every corner of the world arrive on American soil with the promise of a fresh start, and this nation—uniquely designed to embrace diversity—has consistently delivered on that promise.

America's greatness is not merely an accident of history or geography; it is the result of deliberate values and structures that prioritize freedom, individual dignity, and opportunity. At **Di Tran Enterprise**, these same principles drive our mission to empower refugees, strengthen communities, and contribute to the American dream.

This chapter celebrates why America remains the greatest country on Earth, reflecting on the transformative opportunities it offers, the leadership it demonstrates globally, and the essential role refugees play in elevating the nation's strength and prosperity.

The Promise of America: Hope, Opportunity, and Freedom

1. Hope for a Better Tomorrow

For refugees, the decision to leave their homes is never an easy one. It is often born of desperation—a last resort in the face of war, oppression, or economic collapse. Yet, amidst the uncertainty of starting over, America provides hope.

Here, individuals are not defined by their past but by their potential. The United States' commitment to liberty ensures that every person has the opportunity to rise above their circumstances, create a better life, and contribute to society.

2. Unmatched Opportunities

America's economic system is uniquely structured to reward hard work, innovation, and resilience. Refugees, who arrive with little but their determination, find a nation ready to embrace their contributions. From education to entrepreneurship,

America offers pathways for anyone willing to seize the moment.

3. Freedom to Dream and Achieve

In America, freedom is not just a concept—it is a lived reality. The right to speak, worship, and pursue one's goals without fear of persecution is a cornerstone of the American experience. For refugees, this freedom is transformative, unlocking potential that may have been stifled for years.

A Personal Journey: Evidence of America's Promise

My own story as a refugee is a testament to America's greatness. Arriving from Vietnam with no English skills, no resources, and no roadmap for success, I faced challenges that seemed insurmountable. Yet, America became my platform for growth and transformation.

From Struggle to Success

The early years were marked by long hours in factories, nights spent learning a new language, and the slow but steady process of acclimating to an unfamiliar culture. It was hard, but it was possible—and that is the essence of America's promise.

Building a Legacy

Over time, with perseverance and the support of this great nation, I transitioned from an immigrant with limited prospects to an entrepreneur and community leader. Today, through **Di Tran Enterprise**, I dedicate my life to ensuring that others can experience the same journey of transformation.

Paying It Forward

America not only gave me the opportunity to succeed but also the privilege to give back. By empowering refugees through education, workforce development, and community integration, Di Tran Enterprise ensures that the cycle of opportunity continues for generations to come.

Investing in Refugees: A Catalyst for America's Leadership

America's leadership on the global stage is deeply rooted in its ability to attract and empower the best and brightest from around the world. Refugees are

Refugee Resilience:
Elevating Lives, Communities, and America

not just beneficiaries of American generosity—they are contributors to its success.

1. Economic Strength

Refugees bring skills, resilience, and entrepreneurial spirit that drive economic growth. Studies consistently show that refugees are more likely to start businesses than native-born citizens, creating jobs and contributing to local economies.

Example:
Di Tran Enterprise has helped hundreds of refugees launch small businesses, from salons to tech startups. These enterprises not only provide livelihoods but also stimulate economic activity in their communities.

2. Cultural Diversity

America's diversity is one of its greatest assets. Refugees bring unique perspectives, traditions, and innovations that enrich the nation's cultural fabric. This diversity fosters creativity and collaboration, essential for tackling complex global challenges.

Initiatives:
Through cultural integration programs, Di Tran Enterprise ensures that refugees' contributions are celebrated and leveraged for the benefit of all.

Refugee Resilience:
Elevating Lives, Communities, and America

Events like multicultural festivals and storytelling workshops build bridges between communities, reinforcing the idea that diversity is strength.

3. Innovation and Progress

The resilience and resourcefulness of refugees often lead to groundbreaking innovations. From scientific advancements to artistic achievements, refugees have played a pivotal role in shaping America's progress.

Case Study:

A Syrian refugee supported by Di Tran Enterprise recently developed an app connecting local businesses with immigrant workers, streamlining job placement while fostering economic inclusion. This innovation is now being adopted in multiple states.

Challenges to Maximizing Refugee Potential

While America offers unparalleled opportunities, realizing the full potential of refugees requires overcoming significant challenges.

1. Access to Resources

Many refugees lack the immediate resources needed to start their journey toward independence, such as affordable housing, education, and childcare.

Opportunity:

Di Tran Enterprise addresses these gaps by creating integrated support systems that combine housing, training, and mentorship.

---

2. Public Perception

Misinformation and bias can lead to skepticism about refugees' contributions, creating barriers to acceptance and integration.

Opportunity:

By sharing success stories and facilitating community engagement, Di Tran Enterprise helps reshape narratives, highlighting refugees as assets rather than liabilities.

---

3. Policy and Bureaucracy

Complex immigration and resettlement policies can delay access to critical resources, hindering refugees' ability to contribute fully.

Refugee Resilience:
Elevating Lives, Communities, and America

Opportunity:

Di Tran Enterprise advocates for streamlined processes and collaborates with policymakers to create more efficient systems that support both refugees and host communities.

A Multi-Year Blueprint for Empowering Refugees and Elevating America

To harness the potential of refugees and strengthen America's leadership, Di Tran Enterprise has developed a comprehensive multi-year strategy.

Year 1: Foundations of Opportunity

- **Housing and Stability:** Launch affordable housing projects tailored for refugee families, providing a stable foundation for growth.

- **Education and Training:** Expand programs like Louisville Beauty Academy to include technical and healthcare training, addressing labor shortages while empowering participants.

- **Cultural Orientation:** Develop workshops that help refugees navigate American systems and integrate into their communities.

Year 2: Scaling Success

- **Entrepreneurship Support:** Create microloan programs and business incubators to help refugees launch and scale enterprises.

- **Workforce Partnerships:** Collaborate with industries to place refugees in high-demand roles, ensuring a steady pipeline of skilled workers.

- **Community Engagement:** Organize events that celebrate diversity and foster connections between refugees and local residents.

Year 3: Leadership and Legacy

- **Policy Advocacy:** Partner with government agencies to streamline resettlement processes and increase funding for refugee programs.

- **Alumni Networks:** Build a network of program graduates who can mentor new arrivals and advocate for refugee inclusion.

- **National Expansion:** Replicate successful programs in additional regions, creating a scalable model for refugee empowerment.

Strengthening America Through Refugee Empowerment

Empowering refugees is not just an act of compassion—it is a strategic investment in America's future. By welcoming those in need and equipping them to succeed, the United States reinforces its position as a global leader and beacon of hope.

Economic Growth

Refugees contribute billions of dollars to the U.S. economy annually, driving innovation and filling critical workforce gaps.

Social Cohesion

By fostering understanding and collaboration, refugees strengthen the social fabric of their communities, creating a more united and resilient nation.

Global Influence

Refugee Resilience:
Elevating Lives, Communities, and America

America's commitment to refugee resettlement enhances its moral authority and diplomatic standing, demonstrating leadership on the world stage.

Why America Will Always Lead

America's greatness lies in its ability to turn challenges into opportunities, diversity into strength, and adversity into triumph. Refugees are a vital part of this story, bringing new energy, ideas, and determination to a nation built on the promise of a better tomorrow.

At **Di Tran Enterprise**, we are proud to play a role in this transformative journey, ensuring that refugees have the tools they need to succeed and that America remains the land of opportunity for all. With unwavering belief in the principles of *"Yes I CAN"* and *"USA is the #1 country on earth,"* we stand ready to partner with government agencies, communities, and individuals to build a brighter, more inclusive future.

Together, we can ensure that America continues to lead—not just by its power, but by its example. The

Refugee Resilience:
Elevating Lives, Communities, and America

story of refugees is the story of America: one of resilience, possibility, and boundless hope.

Chapter 10: The Future of Refugee Assistance – A National Call to Action

The American promise of opportunity, freedom, and prosperity has always been a beacon for those seeking refuge from turmoil and hardship. As the nation continues to welcome individuals and families fleeing crises, the need for innovative, sustainable refugee assistance programs becomes more pressing than ever. The challenges refugees face are complex, but they also present an unparalleled opportunity for America to reaffirm its leadership on the global stage by demonstrating the transformative power of compassion, collaboration, and inclusion.

Di Tran Enterprise envisions a future where refugee assistance is not only effective but also transformative—a system where those in need today become contributors to the nation's growth and success tomorrow. By fostering seamless partnerships between government agencies, private organizations, and local communities, this vision is not just achievable; it is essential for the continued strength and prosperity of the United States.

Refugee Resilience:
Elevating Lives, Communities, and America

A Vision for Refugee Assistance in America

1. Seamless Public-Private Collaboration

Refugee assistance in America must be built on the foundation of strong partnerships between government agencies and organizations like Di Tran Enterprise. These collaborations leverage the strengths of each sector, combining the government's resources and oversight with the flexibility, innovation, and grassroots connections of private organizations.

Key Elements of Collaboration:

- **Policy Alignment:** Government agencies provide the regulatory framework and funding necessary for large-scale programs, while private organizations ensure these resources are deployed effectively at the community level.

- **Data-Driven Decisions:** Shared data and analytics between public and private entities enable targeted interventions, ensuring programs address the specific needs of refugee populations.

- **Joint Accountability:** Clear metrics and reporting structures ensure that all stakeholders are held accountable for measurable outcomes, fostering trust and transparency.

---

2. A Self-Sustaining Model for Refugee Empowerment

The ultimate goal of refugee assistance should be to create self-sustaining systems that empower individuals to become active contributors to society. This requires a shift from viewing refugees as recipients of aid to recognizing them as partners in building a stronger, more inclusive America.

Core Principles of Self-Sustainability:

- **Economic Integration:** Refugees are provided with the tools, training, and opportunities needed to secure meaningful employment or start businesses.

- **Community Leadership:** Successful refugees are encouraged to take on leadership roles, mentoring others and advocating for policies that support integration.

Refugee Resilience:
Elevating Lives, Communities, and America

- **Generational Impact:** Programs prioritize education and family support, ensuring that future generations are equipped to thrive and contribute.

3. Innovation in Refugee Assistance

As the challenges refugees face evolve, so too must the strategies used to address them. Di Tran Enterprise emphasizes the importance of innovation, using technology, partnerships, and community engagement to create scalable solutions.

Innovative Approaches:

- **Digital Platforms:** Online portals connect refugees with training resources, job opportunities, and support networks, breaking down barriers of time and geography.

- **Mobile Services:** Mobile units deliver healthcare, legal assistance, and education to underserved refugee populations, ensuring access in even the most remote areas.

- **Local Hubs:** Community centers serve as one-stop shops for refugees, providing everything from language classes to mental health counseling under one roof.

Challenges in Refugee Assistance and Opportunities for Growth

The future of refugee assistance in America depends on addressing existing challenges while capitalizing on opportunities for growth and innovation.

Challenge 1: Resource Constraints

Even with government funding, the demand for refugee assistance often exceeds available resources.

Opportunity:

Public-private partnerships allow for the pooling of resources, with private organizations like Di Tran Enterprise attracting additional funding from donors, businesses, and philanthropists.

Challenge 2: Policy and Bureaucracy

Complex regulations and slow-moving processes can delay access to critical services for refugees.

Opportunity:

Streamlining administrative procedures through technology and collaboration reduces delays, ensuring that refugees receive support when they need it most.

Challenge 3: Public Perception

Misinformation and stereotypes about refugees can create resistance to assistance programs.

Opportunity:

By sharing success stories and emphasizing refugees' contributions to the economy and society, organizations like Di Tran Enterprise help shift public perception and build support for resettlement initiatives.

Actionable Steps for Collaboration and Success

To achieve this vision, government agencies, private organizations, and local communities must take specific, coordinated actions.

For Government Agencies:

Refugee Resilience:
Elevating Lives, Communities, and America

- **Increase Funding:** Allocate additional resources to refugee assistance programs, prioritizing those with proven track records of success.

- **Simplify Processes:** Streamline pathways for refugees to access housing, education, and employment, reducing administrative burdens.

- **Promote Public Awareness:** Launch campaigns that highlight the positive impact of refugees on the economy and society.

For Private Organizations:

- **Expand Programs:** Develop initiatives that address gaps in existing services, such as affordable childcare, specialized training, or mental health support.

- **Leverage Technology:** Use digital tools to increase the reach and efficiency of refugee assistance programs.

- **Advocate for Policy Change:** Collaborate with government agencies to advocate for policies that support refugee integration and empowerment.

For Communities:

- **Create Welcoming Environments:** Foster inclusion through cultural exchange events, mentorship programs, and volunteer opportunities.

- **Support Local Businesses:** Encourage the patronage of refugee-owned businesses, strengthening both the local economy and social cohesion.

- **Build Networks:** Establish connections between refugees and community leaders, educators, and employers to facilitate integration.

A Multi-Year Strategy for Refugee Assistance

Di Tran Enterprise has developed a comprehensive multi-year strategy to lead the future of refugee assistance in America.

Year 1: Foundations of Partnership

Refugee Resilience:
Elevating Lives, Communities, and America

- Establish partnerships with government agencies, businesses, and community organizations to create a unified approach to refugee assistance.

- Launch pilot programs in housing, education, and workforce development to identify best practices.

- Build a digital platform to connect refugees with resources and opportunities.

Year 2: Scaling Success

- Expand successful pilot programs to additional regions, focusing on areas with high refugee populations.

- Introduce mobile units and virtual services to increase accessibility for underserved communities.

- Develop specialized programs for vulnerable groups, such as unaccompanied minors or elderly refugees.

Year 3: National Leadership

Refugee Resilience:
Elevating Lives, Communities, and America

- Advocate for policy changes at the federal level, using data and success stories to influence decision-making.

- Transition program graduates into leadership roles, creating a network of refugee mentors and advocates.

- Establish a national model for refugee assistance that can be replicated by other organizations.

The Role of Di Tran Enterprise in Shaping the Future

Di Tran Enterprise is uniquely positioned to lead the transformation of refugee assistance in America. With a proven track record in workforce development, housing, education, and community integration, the organization serves as a model for how public-private partnerships can create lasting change.

Through innovative programs, strategic collaboration, and an unwavering commitment to results, Di Tran Enterprise demonstrates that empowering refugees is not just a moral imperative—it is a strategic investment in America's future.

A Heartfelt Call to Action

The future of refugee assistance depends on the collective efforts of policymakers, business leaders, community members, and organizations like Di Tran Enterprise. By working together, we can build a system that honors America's legacy as a land of opportunity while addressing the challenges of today's world.

This is a call to action—for government agencies to invest boldly, for businesses to innovate responsibly, and for communities to embrace inclusivity. It is a call to believe in the transformative power of collaboration and to recognize that every refugee we empower strengthens the fabric of our nation.

America is at its greatest when it leads with compassion, courage, and conviction. By empowering refugees, we reaffirm our values, enhance our economy, and secure our place as a global leader. Together, we can create a future where refugees are not just surviving but thriving, contributing to a stronger, more united America.

Refugee Resilience:
Elevating Lives, Communities, and America

The time to act is now. Join us in building a brighter future for refugees, for America, and for generations to come. Together, we can turn challenges into opportunities and dreams into reality.

Summary Chapter: Top 10 Challenges Refugees Face and How Di Tran Enterprise Can Partner with Government Agencies to Provide Scalable Solutions

Refugees bring resilience, skills, and determination to the United States, but their journey to integration is filled with challenges that require innovative and collaborative solutions. **Di Tran Enterprise**, with its proven expertise in empowering refugees, stands ready to partner with government agencies to address these challenges at scale. By leveraging federal, state, and city-level funding, Di Tran Enterprise offers a sustainable model to transform refugee support systems into engines of empowerment, ensuring that refugees transition from recipients of aid to contributors to the nation's growth.

Below, we outline the top 10 challenges refugees face and the corresponding solutions, funding opportunities, and steps for agencies to collaborate with Di Tran Enterprise to implement these programs effectively.

---

1. Housing Shortages

Challenge:

Refugees often struggle to find affordable, safe, and stable housing, with many living in overcrowded or substandard conditions.

Solution:

- Develop affordable housing using **HUD's Community Development Block Grant (CDBG)** and **HOME Investment Partnerships Program** funds.

- Launch transitional housing programs funded through **Emergency Solutions Grants (ESG)**.

- Create pathways to homeownership with support from state-level **Housing Trust Funds** and city-specific initiatives like local **Housing Finance Agencies (HFAs)**.

Steps for Application:

Refugee Resilience:

Elevating Lives, Communities, and America

1. Work with HUD regional offices to apply for CDBG and HOME funding.

2. Partner with state housing departments to identify specific housing needs and align with available grants.

3. Collaborate with local city councils to secure HFAs funding and ensure zoning approval for housing projects.

Agency Partnership Pitch:

Di Tran Enterprise is an ideal partner for implementing scalable housing solutions. Our expertise in combining public and private investments ensures efficient and impactful housing development, creating stability for refugee families.

---

2. Language Barriers

Challenge:

Limited English proficiency hinders refugees' ability to integrate, access resources, and secure employment.

Solution:

Refugee Resilience:
Elevating Lives, Communities, and America

- Deliver language programs using **Office of Refugee Resettlement (ORR)** funds and **Workforce Innovation and Opportunity Act (WIOA)** grants.

- Establish bilingual mentorship programs supported by state-level immigrant services grants.

- Collaborate with city libraries and education departments to deliver ESL classes funded by local community budgets.

Steps for Application:

1. Submit grant proposals to ORR and state-level workforce development agencies for language training programs.

2. Partner with local community centers and libraries to access city-level education funds.

3. Design a curriculum tailored to workforce needs, enhancing both language skills and job readiness.

Agency Partnership Pitch:
Di Tran Enterprise specializes in integrating practical language instruction with mentorship, ensuring

Refugee Resilience:
Elevating Lives, Communities, and America

refugees develop the skills needed for rapid integration and workforce success.

---

3. Employment Struggles

Challenge:

Refugees face challenges entering the workforce due to a lack of professional networks, unrecognized credentials, and cultural unfamiliarity.

Solution:

- Create workforce training programs funded by **ORR's Refugee Career Pathways Program** and **WIOA's Adult and Dislocated Worker Program**.

- Develop employer partnerships supported by state-level economic development grants and wage subsidy programs.

- Establish job placement programs through city workforce development boards.

Steps for Application:

1. Apply for ORR workforce development grants, emphasizing skills training for high-demand industries.

Refugee Resilience:
Elevating Lives, Communities, and America

2. Collaborate with local economic development agencies to build employer relationships.

3. Use city workforce boards to create job fairs and employer matchmaking events.

Agency Partnership Pitch:

Di Tran Enterprise bridges the gap between refugees and employers through tailored training programs, ensuring rapid and meaningful workforce integration.

---

4. Unrecognized Skills and Credentials

Challenge:

Refugees with valuable professional experience often cannot use their credentials in the U.S., limiting career opportunities.

Solution:

- Implement re-certification programs using **ORR funding** and **Perkins Career and Technical Education grants**.

- Develop skills assessment workshops supported by state labor department grants.

Refugee Resilience:
Elevating Lives, Communities, and America

- Offer professional development courses funded by local immigrant inclusion grants.

Steps for Application:

1. Work with licensing boards and professional associations to streamline re-certification processes.

2. Partner with state workforce boards to design skill alignment assessments.

3. Secure funding from city-level immigrant inclusion initiatives to expand upskilling workshops.

Agency Partnership Pitch:

Di Tran Enterprise excels at connecting refugees' skills with U.S. labor market demands, ensuring their talents are recognized and utilized effectively.

---

5. Isolation and Lack of Community Integration

Challenge:

Cultural differences and limited social networks can leave refugees feeling disconnected and unsupported.

Solution:

Refugee Resilience:
Elevating Lives, Communities, and America

- Use **ORR's Refugee Social Services (RSS)** funding to organize cultural orientation workshops.

- Host community engagement events funded by city arts councils and local government grants.

- Develop mentorship programs using state-level immigrant support grants.

Steps for Application:

1. Apply for RSS funding to design and deliver cultural integration programs.

2. Partner with city arts councils to host multicultural events.

3. Work with state agencies to fund mentorship and community connection initiatives.

Agency Partnership Pitch:

Di Tran Enterprise fosters meaningful community connections, ensuring refugees feel welcome and integrated into their new environments.

---

6. Mental Health Challenges

Challenge:

Refugee Resilience:
Elevating Lives, Communities, and America

Trauma, stress, and anxiety from past experiences and resettlement challenges affect refugees' well-being.

Solution:

- Provide trauma-informed counseling using **SAMHSA (Substance Abuse and Mental Health Services Administration)** grants.

- Establish peer support groups funded by state mental health initiatives.

- Launch mobile mental health units using city public health funding.

Steps for Application:

1. Apply for SAMHSA grants to support mental health services for refugees.

2. Partner with state mental health departments to expand peer counseling programs.

3. Secure local funding to deploy mobile health units in underserved areas.

Agency Partnership Pitch:

Di Tran Enterprise combines culturally sensitive counseling with innovative delivery models, ensuring refugees receive the mental health support they need.

---

7. Access to Education

Challenge:

Refugees often face barriers to education due to language limitations, financial constraints, and unfamiliar systems.

Solution:

- Use **Title III funds** under the Elementary and Secondary Education Act to support English learners in schools.

- Provide adult education programs funded by **WIOA Title II**.

- Create scholarship opportunities supported by state education departments and city immigrant inclusion funds.

Steps for Application:

1. Work with school districts to apply for Title III funding.

Refugee Resilience:
Elevating Lives, Communities, and America

2. Partner with state education departments to access WIOA Title II grants.

3. Collaborate with local governments to design scholarship programs for refugee students.

Agency Partnership Pitch:
Di Tran Enterprise ensures refugee families access quality education, building a foundation for multi-generational success.

---

8. Limited Access to Healthcare

Challenge:

Refugees face difficulties accessing affordable healthcare due to lack of insurance, unfamiliarity with the system, and cultural barriers.

Solution:

- Launch health literacy programs using **HRSA (Health Resources and Services Administration)** funds.

- Establish refugee-specific clinics supported by **Refugee Health Promotion Program** grants.

Refugee Resilience:
Elevating Lives, Communities, and America

- Deploy mobile health units funded by state and city health department grants.

Steps for Application:

1. Apply for HRSA grants to fund healthcare navigation programs.

2. Partner with state health departments to create clinics tailored to refugee needs.

3. Secure local public health funding to deploy mobile units in underserved areas.

Agency Partnership Pitch:

Di Tran Enterprise creates accessible healthcare solutions tailored to refugee communities, ensuring well-being and productivity.

---

9. Financial Instability

Challenge:

Refugees often arrive with little financial security, making it difficult to meet basic needs or invest in their futures.

Solution:

Refugee Resilience:
Elevating Lives, Communities, and America

- Use **Temporary Assistance for Needy Families (TANF)** funds to provide short-term financial aid.

- Offer microloans supported by state economic development grants.

- Deliver financial literacy programs funded by local community foundations.

Steps for Application:

1. Collaborate with TANF offices to secure funding for emergency support.

2. Partner with state economic agencies to establish microloan programs.

3. Apply for local grants to deliver financial literacy workshops.

Agency Partnership Pitch:
Di Tran Enterprise empowers refugees to achieve financial stability through tailored support and education.

---

10. Building Long-Term Independence

Challenge:

Refugee Resilience:
Elevating Lives, Communities, and America

Many refugee programs focus on short-term needs, neglecting long-term pathways to independence.

Solution:

- Design entrepreneurship programs using **Small Business Administration (SBA)** grants.

- Establish leadership development initiatives funded by state workforce boards.

- Create alumni mentorship networks supported by city immigrant services grants.

Steps for Application:

1. Apply for SBA funding to create refugee entrepreneur incubators.

2. Partner with state workforce boards to fund leadership training programs.

3. Use city grants to support alumni-driven mentorship initiatives.

Agency Partnership Pitch:
Di Tran Enterprise ensures refugees transition from recipients of aid to leaders, entrepreneurs, and active contributors to America's growth.

Refugee Resilience:
Elevating Lives, Communities, and America

The End

Thank You

"Refugee assistance is not just about providing aid; it's about unlocking potential, building bridges, and creating pathways for resilience to thrive. When we say, 'YES I CAN,' we affirm that every refugee is a partner in progress, every challenge is an opportunity for growth, and every step forward strengthens the fabric of America—the greatest country on Earth."
– Di Tran